# Contents

| | |
|---|---|
| Australia is a continent | 4 |
| Early Australia | 6 |
| Australia today | 8 |
| The land | 10 |
| The climate | 12 |
| Plants and animals | 14 |
| The people | 16 |
| Australia's states | 18 |

**Regions**

| | |
|---|---|
| The Pacific | 20 |
| Australia | 21 |
| New Zealand | 22 |
| South Pacific Islands | 24 |
| Melanesia | 26 |
| Australia's future | 28 |
| Australia in review | 30 |
| Websites | 30 |
| Glossary | 31 |
| Index | 32 |

## Glossary words

When a word is printed in **bold**, you can look up its meaning in the Glossary on page 31.

# Australia is a continent

Australia is the smallest continent in the world. Look at a world map or globe and you can see the world is made up of water and land. The big areas of land are called continents. There are seven continents:

- Africa
- Antarctica
- Asia
- Australia
- Europe
- North America
- South America.

## Borders

The borders of continents follow natural physical features such as coastlines and mountain ranges. Australia is the world's largest island, so its borders are all oceans and seas. These are Australia's sea borders:

- Arafura Sea
- Coral Sea
- Indian Ocean
- Pacific Ocean
- Southern Ocean
- Tasman Sea
- Timor Sea

 World map showing the seven modern-day continents

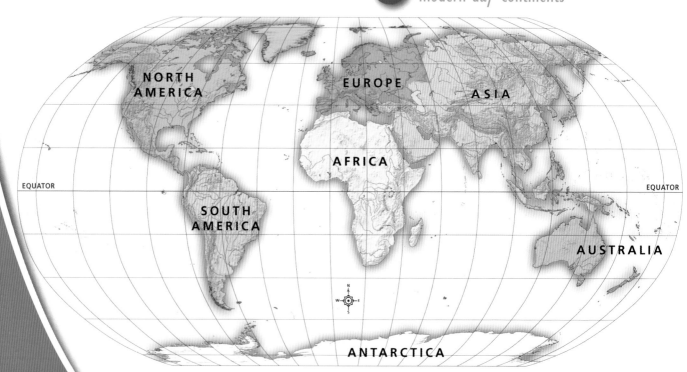

NORTH AMERICA

EUROPE

ASIA

AFRICA

EQUATOR

EQUATOR

SOUTH AMERICA

AUSTRALIA

ANTARCTICA

# The world is a jigsaw

The Earth's crust is made up of huge plates, called **tectonic plates**, which fit together like a jigsaw puzzle. These plates are constantly moving, up and down and sideways, up to 10 centimetres (4 inches) a year. Over long periods of time, the plates change in size and shape as their edges push against each other.

Around 250 million years ago, there was one massive supercontinent called Pangaea. Around 200 million years ago it began splitting and formed two continents. Laurasia was the northern continent and Gondwana was the southern continent. By about 65 million years ago, Laurasia and Gondwana had separated into smaller landmasses that look much like the continents we know today. Laurasia split to form Europe, Asia and North America. Gondwana split to form South America, Africa, Australia and Antarctica.

Australia was once part of the supercontinent Pangaea.

The Australian continent formed when Gondwana split into smaller landmasses.

# Early Australia

When the continents were one, animals moved across the land, as there was no water to stop them. When the continents split apart, the animals were left on separate landmasses and they began to change and develop into the animals we know today. During this time dinosaurs roamed the Earth. As dinosaurs became **extinct**, other animals replaced them. Many of these animals in Australia were **marsupials**. The diprotodon was a gigantic marsupial that looked like an oversized **wombat**. It was 3 metres (10 feet) long and ate plants. Giant kangaroos also roamed Australia and grew to over 3 metres (10 feet) tall. These animals also died out or became extinct, but other animals survived to become the kangaroos, possums and wombats that live in Australia today.

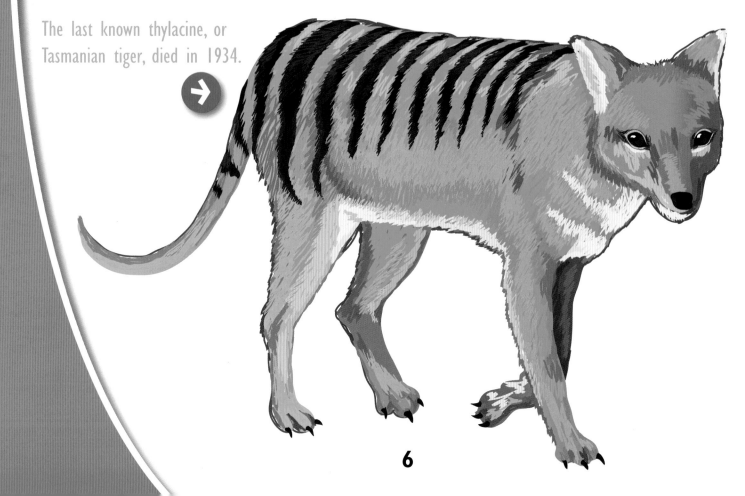

The last known thylacine, or Tasmanian tiger, died in 1934.

# Early humans

Scientists believe modern humans, or *Homo sapiens*, came from Africa then made their way across Asia to Australia about 40 000 years ago. Scientists believe this because they tested the age of simple stone tools found in the areas where these people lived. The people who made these tools were the **ancestors** of the Australian Aboriginal people. The Aboriginal people lived all over the continent in hundreds of separate tribes or groups. Many of these tribes spoke different languages. The Aboriginal people moved around their land looking for food. They hunted animals and gathered fruits, plants and seeds from the bush. Aboriginal people living near the coast fished and collected seafood. They painted on cave walls and rocks about their lives and beliefs.

↑ These ancient stone axes were found in a dry lake in Western Australia.

↓ The Wandjina Paintings are on the Mitchell Plateau in the Kimberley, Western Australia.

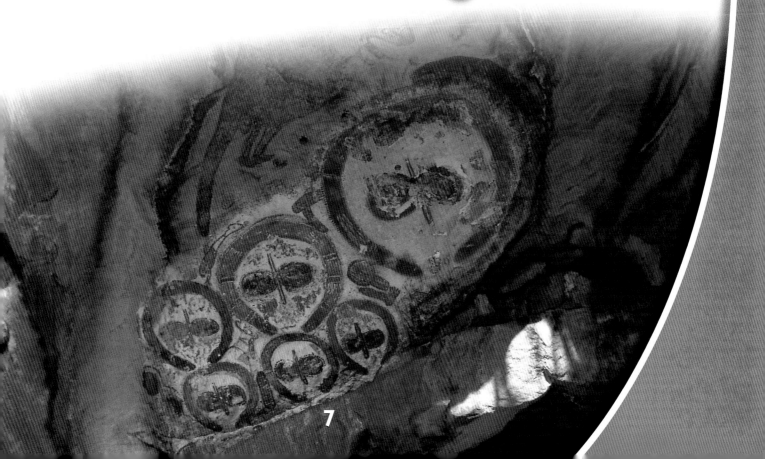

# Australia today

Australia is the smallest continent at 7 686 850 square kilometres (2 967 893 square miles). Australia is the only continent made up of just one country. All other continents have more than one country within their borders. Australia is divided into six states:

- New South Wales
- Queensland
- South Australia
- Tasmania
- Victoria
- Western Australia.

There are also two territories:

- Australian Capital Territory
- Northern Territory.

↓ The physical features of Australia

↑ Chambers Pillar is in the centre of Australia.

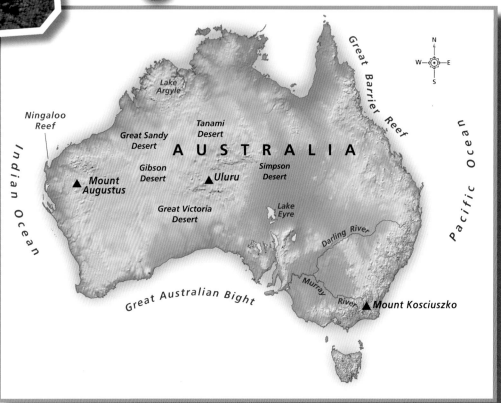

8

 There are many white sandy beaches along Australia's coastline.

## Physical features

Australia is in the **Southern Hemisphere**. Australia is a land with many different physical features. The coastline ranges from white sandy beaches and rugged cliffs to muddy **mangroves**. The middle of Australia is dry desert. A series of mountains stretch down near to the eastern coast. Rivers flow across the country to the coast or to inland lakes.

## Australian people

Australia's Indigenous people are the Aboriginals and **Torres Strait Islanders**. Around 230 years ago the British came to the region, bringing with them their own traditions, language and religion. During the last 100 years, many **migrants** from China and parts of Europe such as Greece and Italy have settled in Australia. Since the 1970s, more migrants from Asia have come to Australia to live. Many of them have come from Vietnam.

This Aboriginal child in Northern Australia is showing a group of city children an edible root.

# The land

Australia's landscape is flat compared to other continents. The only big mountains in Australia are in New South Wales, Victoria and Tasmania.

## Mountains

The highest mountain in Australia is Mount Kosciuszko at 2229 metres (7313 feet). Mount Kosciuszko is in the Snowy Mountains, which are part of the Great Dividing Range or Eastern Highlands. This mountain range runs along the eastern side of the continent from northern Queensland to Tasmania.

Cradle Mountain is in Tasmania

## Biggest rock

Mount Augustus in Western Australia is the biggest rock in the world. It is made up of many layers of rock. Uluru (previously known as Ayers Rock) in the Northern Territory is the biggest monolith or single piece of rock in the world.

Mount Augustus is believed to be 1650 million years old.

## Deserts

Australia has the second largest area of deserts in the world after the Sahara in Africa. The deserts in Australia are:

- Gibson Desert
- Great Sandy Desert
- Great Victoria Desert
- Simpson Desert
- Tanami Desert.

↑ The Darling River in New South Wales

## Rivers

The longest river in Australia is the Murray–Darling River system at 3750 kilometres (2330 miles) long. The Darling River joins the Murray River in New South Wales and flows to the coast in South Australia.

## Lakes

Lake Eyre in South Australia is the largest lake in Australia. Lake Eyre is usually dry, only filling with water after heavy rains. This happens approximately every 30 years. When the Ord River in the north of Western Australia was dammed, it formed a huge man-made lake called Lake Argyle.

## Coral reefs

Coral reefs extend along parts of northern Australia and surround some islands. The Great Barrier Reef stretches along the east coast of Australia. Ningaloo Reef is off Western Australia.

### Longest coral reef

The Great Barrier Reef is the longest coral reef in the world. It is about 2500 kilometres (1550 miles) long. Coral is actually billions of small creatures called polyps that together form the reef.

↓ A turtle on Ningaloo Reef in Western Australia

# The climate

**B**eing in the Southern Hemisphere, Australia's summer is from December to February and winter is from June to August. Australia is the second driest continent after Antarctica.

## Arid climate

Australia's deserts have an **arid** climate with very hot summers and little rain. In winter the temperature can drop to below 0°C (32°F) at night. Australian deserts are very dry places but sometimes a rare thunderstorm brings heavy rain and floods.

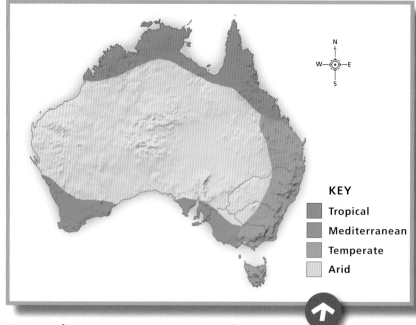

KEY
- Tropical
- Mediterranean
- Temperate
- Arid

Climate zones in Australia

### Hottest town

Marble Bar in Western Australia is Australia's hottest town. Temperatures there often reach more than 42°C (108°F).

## Mediterranean climate

Southern parts of Western Australia near Perth and South Australia near Adelaide have a **Mediterranean** climate with hot dry summers and cool wet winters.

Wind creates the rippled pattern on these desert sand dunes in western New South Wales.

## Tropical monsoon climate

Northern Australia has a **tropical** monsoon climate. In summer, the weather is hot with heavy rain falling on most days. In winter, temperatures are cooler with little rain. Further south the climate becomes sub-tropical with slightly drier, cooler weather. Both Brisbane and Sydney have a sub-tropical climate. Northern parts of Australia also experience cyclones (hurricanes) during summer.

## Temperate climate

South-eastern Australia, including most of Victoria, Tasmania and parts of New South Wales, have warm summers and cool, even cold, winters. Rain can fall any time of the year. Melbourne and Hobart have a **temperate** climate.

## Alpine climate

Mountainous parts of Tasmania, New South Wales and Victoria get enough snow in winter to allow people to ski. This is known as an **alpine** climate.

# Plants and animals

Australia has a wide range of animals, birds, reptiles and flowering plants. Many of these plants and animals are found nowhere else in the world.

## Forests

The eucalyptus tree comes from Australia. There are many different types of eucalyptus trees.

Many of Australia's marsupials live in eucalyptus forests. Koalas and possums live high up in the branches of these trees. While koalas eat only certain types of eucalyptus leaves, such as the manna gum, possums like fruits, insects and sometimes birds' eggs. Birds such as budgerigars and cockatoos nest in the holes of eucalyptus trees.

## Monotremes

Two animals from the monotremes group live in Australia. Monotremes are the only **mammals** that lay eggs. The platypus lives in streams and eats freshwater crayfish. It has a bill like a duck, webbed feet and a furry body. The echidna looks like a large hedgehog and uses its long tongue to catch ants to eat.

If frightened, echidnas roll up into a ball with their spikes facing outwards.

Tall karri eucalyptus trees grow in the wet south-west of Western Australia.

## Desert

In the dry regions animals and plants learn to live under hot and dry conditions. When it does rain small plants produce seeds in a short time. These seeds can lie on the dry ground for months or even years before the next rains come.

Kangaroos live in both forests and deserts. The red kangaroo prefers drier places where it eats grasses. It can grow to 1.8 metres (6 feet) tall and jump 6.4 metres (21 feet) in a single leap. Some reptiles such as snakes and lizards live in the desert. They eat insects and small marsupial mice.

Plants called everlastings bloom after rare desert rains.

## Rainforest

The tropical rainforest grows in northern Queensland where there is high rainfall. Some trees grow tall and close together shading the plants below.

# The people

Aboriginal people fishing from a river in northern Australia.

**A**ustralia has the least people of any continent except for Antarctica. There are 20 million people living in Australia. Some big cities in Asia and South America have nearly as many people living in them as the whole of Australia.

## Ethnic groups

Aboriginal and Torres Strait Islander peoples make up only a small amount of Australia's population today. Most people in Australia are ancestors of settlers from the United Kingdom, Europe and Asia. During the 1950s and 1960s, thousands of people came to Australia as migrants. They came mainly from the United Kingdom and Europe. Today, many people from Asian countries, New Zealand and South Africa are making Australia their home. This mix of people living together is called a multicultural society.

## Languages

Before people from the United Kingdom settled in Australia, Aboriginal and Torres Strait Islander peoples spoke at least 200 separate languages. English is now the official language of Australia. Many Indigenous people also speak their traditional languages. People living in Australia have developed their own English words such as:

⊕ billabong (a waterhole)

⊕ brumby (a wild horse)

⊕ digger (an Australian soldier).

Many Asian and European migrants also speak the languages of their homelands.

## Religion

Before the Europeans arrived, the Aboriginal tribes followed their own beliefs which were part of the **Dreamtime**. Aboriginal people in Australia believe spirits made all the rocks, water, plants and animals in the world. When Europeans came to Australia, they brought the Christian religion with them. Although Aboriginal people still follow their old beliefs many also follow Christianity. Migrants introduced other religions such as **Buddhism**, **Hinduism**, **Judaism** and **Islam**.

Many Christians in Australia go to church on Sundays.

# Australia's states

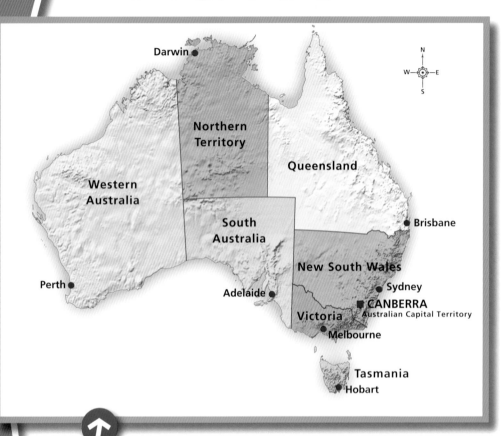

Australian states and territories, including major cities

Australia has six states and two territories. Most Australians live on the east coast of the continent in Queensland, New South Wales, Victoria and the Australian Capital Territory. Western Australia, South Australia and the Northern Territory have large areas of desert and are less populated. Tasmania has the smallest population of all the states.

## Colonies

When Captain James Cook landed in Botany Bay in New South Wales in 1776, he declared Australia a part of, or a colony of, Britain. Soon after, people from Britain sailed out to Australia and settled on the land. While some came as free settlers, others were convicts or prisoners from overcrowded gaols in Britain. These new Australian settlements were called colonies. The settlers cleared areas of land for farms and built towns. They built their homes and buildings in the same style as they had back in their homeland. Australia still has some buildings from this period.

## Land ownership

The Aboriginal people have a close connection to the land where they come from. When the British arrived in Australia, many Aboriginal people lost their land to towns and farms. Some Aboriginal people are now getting back their traditional lands through land rights reforms. Many Aboriginal people also live in Australia's country towns, cities and settlements.

## World War II invasion

Australia has been a mainly peaceful place with no big battles fought on its home soil. This nearly changed during World War II (1939–45) when the Japanese took over the Pacific Islands and invaded Papua New Guinea (PNG). Australian and New Zealand troops fought the Japanese in PNG and the Pacific. The Australian towns of Darwin and Broome were bombed. With the help of American forces, Japan was defeated in 1945.

 These Aboriginal people are performing a welcoming ceremony to their land.

# The Pacific

The Pacific region covers 8.5 million square kilometres (3.3 million square miles) of the Pacific Ocean and its islands. Including Australia, there are 14 **independent** countries in the Pacific.

The regions and countries of the Pacific

# Australia

| Country | Languages | Religions | Ethnic groups | Agriculture | Natural resources |
|---------|-----------|-----------|---------------|-------------|-------------------|
| Australia | ■ ■ ● ■ ☐ | ✝ ☪ ✡ ☼ | 🧍 🧍 🧍 | ❖ ☐ ♣ ☆ ✪ ✪ | ◆◆◆◆◆◆◆◆ ◆◆◆◆●◆ |

| Key | Languages | Religions | Ethnic groups | Agriculture | Natural resources |
|-----|-----------|-----------|---------------|-------------|-------------------|
| | ■ Aboriginal languages <br> ■ English <br> ● Mandarin Chinese <br> ■ Traditional languages <br> ☐ Vietnamese | ✝ Christian <br> ☪ Islam <br> ✡ Jewish <br> ☼ Traditional beliefs | 🧍 Aboriginal <br> 🧍 Asian <br> 🧍 European | ❖ Cereal grains <br> ✪ Citrus <br> ✪ Dairy <br> ♣ Fruit and vegetables <br> ☆ Sheep, cattle and goats <br> ☐ Sugar cane | ◆ Bauxite or Alumina <br> ◆ Coal <br> ◆ Copper <br> ◆ Diamonds <br> ◆ Gold <br> ◆ **Hydropower** <br> ◆ Iron ore <br> ◆ Lead <br> ◆ Nickel <br> ● Oil and gas <br> ◆ Silver <br> ◆ Timber <br> ◆ Tin <br> ◆ Uranium <br> ◆ Zinc |

## Australia in focus

**Official name:** Commonwealth of Australia

**Area:** 7 686 850 square kilometres (2 967 893 square miles)

**Population:** 20 million

**Capital:** Canberra

**Major cities:** Sydney, Melbourne, Brisbane, Perth, Adelaide, Hobart, Darwin

**Colonial rule:** England

**Famous landmarks:** Sydney Harbour Bridge, Sydney Opera House, Uluru (Ayers Rock), Great Australian Bight, Great Barrier Reef, the **outback**

**Famous people:** Nicole Kidman, Mel Gibson (actors), Don Bradman (cricketer)

**Traditions:** Australian Rules football, cricket

**Traditional food:** **bush tucker**, barbecues, pavlova, lamingtons, meat pie and sauce

The Sydney Opera House and the Sydney Harbour Bridge in Sydney, the capital city of New South Wales.

Australia's land size makes it the sixth largest country in the world. Sydney is Australia's most populated city with more than 4 million people. Tourism and mining are Australia's biggest money earners. Australia is rich in natural **resources**, especially minerals such as iron ore, gold and coal. Wool, wheat and beef are Australia's biggest agricultural industries.

# New Zealand

New Zealand is part of the Pacific Islands and lies about 2012 kilometres south-east of Australia. It is located in the Pacific Ocean and is south of the equator in the Southern Hemisphere. New Zealand consists of two large islands and many smaller islands. The North Island and South Island make up almost the entire area of the country and are separated by Cook Strait. Of the inhabited islands, Stewart Island is the next largest after the North and South Islands. The South Island contains Mount Cook, which is the highest point in New Zealand.

| Country | Languages | Religions | Ethnic groups | Agriculture | Natural resources |
|---|---|---|---|---|---|
| New Zealand | ■ ■ | ✝ | 👤 👤 👤 👤 | ✣ ♣ ☆ ✪ | ♦ ♦ ♦ ◈ ◈ ◈ |

| Key | Languages | Religions | Ethnic groups | Agriculture | Natural resources |
|---|---|---|---|---|---|
| | ■ English<br>■ Maori languages | ✝ Christian | 👤 Asian<br>👤 European<br>👤 Maori<br>👤 Pacific Islander | ✣ Cereal grains<br>✪ Dairy<br>♣ Fruit and vegetables<br>☆ Sheep, cattle and goats | ♦ Coal<br>◈ Gold<br>◈ Hydropower<br>♦ Iron ore<br>● Oil and gas<br>◈ Timber |

# New Zealand in focus

**Official name:** New Zealand

**Area:** 268 680 square kilometres (103 737 square miles)

**Population:** 4 million

**Capital:** Wellington

**Major cities:** Auckland, Christchurch, Dunedin, Hamilton

**Colonial rule:** England

**Famous landmarks:** Mount Cook, New Zealand's highest mountain at 3764 metres (12 349 feet), Mount Ruapehu, Rotorua

**Famous people:** Russell Crowe, Sam Neil (actors), Dame Kiri Te Kanawa (opera singer)

**Traditions:** Rugby Union, haka (Maori dance)

**Traditional food:** kumara (sweet potato), whitebait (fritters of tiny fish), trout, hangi (food steamed in a pit on hot rocks)

Wellington is the capital city of New Zealand.

New Zealand is a very scenic country with snow-capped mountains, green fields and big lakes. There are two main islands, the North Island and the South Island. New Zealand also includes smaller islands such as Stewart Island. More New Zealanders live on the North Island than the South Island.

This mountainous country is on the South Island of New Zealand.

# South Pacific Islands

There are eight South Pacific Island countries. Use the key below to find out about and compare each country's languages, religions, ethnic groups, agriculture and natural resources.

| Country | Languages | Religions | Ethnic groups | Agriculture | Natural resources |
|---|---|---|---|---|---|
| Vanuatu | ■ ■ ■ ■ | ✝ ✲ | 👤 👤 👤 | ◐ ■ ✳ ❖ ☆ | ◆ ◆ |
| Tuvalu | ■ ■ | ✝ | 👤 👤 | ◐ | |
| Fiji | ■ ■ ■ | ✝ ✿ ☾ | 👤 👤 👤 | ▢ ◐ ❖ ❖ ☆ | ◈ ◈ ◆ ◆ |
| Tonga | ■ ■ | ✝ | 👤 | ◐ ❖ ■ ✳ ✳ | |
| Samoa | ■ ■ | ✝ | 👤 | ◐ ❖ | ◈ ◆ |
| Kiribati | ■ ■ | ✝ | 👤 👤 | ◐ ❖ | ◆ |
| Cook Islands | ■ ■ | ✝ | 👤 👤 | ◐ ❖ ✲ | |
| Niue | ■ ■ | ✝ | 👤 | ◐ ❖ | |

| Key | Languages | Religions | Ethnic groups | Agriculture | Natural resources |
|---|---|---|---|---|---|
| | ■ English | ✝ Christian | 👤 European | ❖ Cereal grains | ◈ Copper |
| | Fijian | ☾ Islam | 👤 Asian | ✲ Citrus | ◈ Gold |
| | ■ French | ✿ Hindu | 👤 French | ■ Cocoa | ◇ Hydropower |
| | Hindustani | ✲ Traditional beliefs | Indian | ✳ Coffee | ◆ Manganese |
| | Pidgin | | 👤 Melanesian | ◐ Coconuts | ◆ Phosphates |
| | ■ Traditional languages | | Micronesian | ❖ Fruit and vegetables | ◈ Timber |
| | | | 👤 Polynesian | ✳ Black pepper | |
| | | | | ☆ Sheep, cattle and goats | |
| | | | | ▢ Sugar cane | |

# Vanuatu in focus

**Official name:** Republic of Vanuatu

**Area:** 14760 square kilometres
(5699 square miles)

**Population:** 198000

**Capital:** Port Vila

**Major cities:** Luganville

**Colonial rule:** France, England

**Famous landmarks:** Yasur Volcano
on Tana Island

**Famous people:** Edward Natapei (political leader),
Philippe Metois (photographer)

**Traditions:** Naghol (people jumping off a 20-metre (80-foot) platform with only
vine rope tied around their feet to break the fall) on Pentecost Island, playing Tamtam
drums and blowing into conch shells

**Traditional food:** yams, manioc, taro, fish, kava (a drink)

This is an active
volcano on Tanna
Island, Vanuatu.

Vanuatu is a group of 13 islands and 70 smaller islands called islets. Some of the
islands are volcanic and others are **coral atolls**. The capital, Port Vila, is on the island
of Éfaté. For many years Vanuatu was ruled by both England and France.

# Fiji in focus

**Official name:** Republic of Fiji

**Area:** 18270 square kilometres (7054 square miles)

**Population:** 850000

**Capital:** Suva

**Major cities:** Lautoka, Nadi, Savusavu

**Colonial rule:** England

**Famous landmarks:** Sigatoka sand dunes,
many white beaches

**Famous people:** Mahendra Chauhdry (first Indian
Prime Minister of Fiji)

**Traditions:** kava (a drink), Mekes (dances),
tapa (cloth making), woodcarving

**Traditional food:** lovo (Fijian feast of roast pork), pumpkin, sweet potato

These Fijian children
live in a small
village.

The country of Fiji is made of more than 800 islands and islets. Some are
tiny with only around 100 people living on them. Some islands are volcanic
with mountains and others have sandy beaches with palm trees. In 1879,
The English brought Indian people in to work on the sugar farms. Today
there are almost as many Indians as Fijians living in Fiji.

# Melanesia

There are six countries in Melanesia. Use the key below to find out about and compare each country's languages, religions, ethnic groups, agriculture and natural resources.

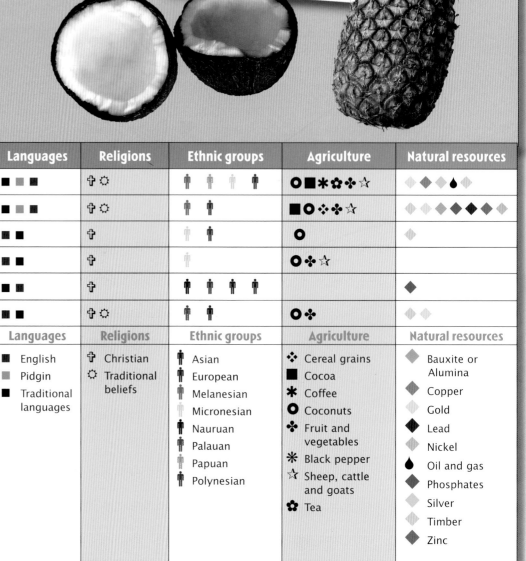

| Country | Languages | Religions | Ethnic groups | Agriculture | Natural resources |
|---|---|---|---|---|---|
| Papua New Guinea | ■ ■ ■ | ✞ ☼ | 🚹 🚹 🚹 🚹 | O ■ ✱ ✿ ✤ ☆ | ◆ ◆ ◆ 🌢 ◆ |
| Solomon Islands | ■ ■ ■ | ✞ ☼ | 🚹 🚹 | ■ O ⁘ ✤ ☆ | ◆ ◆ ◆ ◆ ◆ ◆ ◆ |
| Micronesia | ■ ■ | ✞ | 🚹 🚹 | O | ◆ |
| Marshall Islands | ■ ■ | ✞ | 🚹 | O ✤ ☆ | |
| Nauru | ■ ■ | ✞ | 🚹 🚹 🚹 🚹 | | ◆ |
| Palau | ■ ■ | ✞ ☼ | 🚹 🚹 | O ✤ | ◆ ◆ |

**Key**

| Languages | Religions | Ethnic groups | Agriculture | Natural resources |
|---|---|---|---|---|
| ■ English<br>■ Pidgin<br>■ Traditional languages | ✞ Christian<br>☼ Traditional beliefs | 🚹 Asian<br>🚹 European<br>🚹 Melanesian<br>🚹 Micronesian<br>🚹 Nauruan<br>🚹 Palauan<br>🚹 Papuan<br>🚹 Polynesian | ⁘ Cereal grains<br>■ Cocoa<br>✱ Coffee<br>O Coconuts<br>✤ Fruit and vegetables<br>✳ Black pepper<br>☆ Sheep, cattle and goats<br>✿ Tea | ◆ Bauxite or Alumina<br>◆ Copper<br>◆ Gold<br>◆ Lead<br>◆ Nickel<br>🌢 Oil and gas<br>◆ Phosphates<br>◆ Silver<br>◆ Timber<br>◆ Zinc |

# Papua New Guinea in focus

**Official name:** Independent State of Papua New Guinea

**Area:** 461 690 square kilometres (178 258 square miles)

**Population:** 5.3 million

**Capital:** Port Moresby

**Major cities:** Lae, Madang

**Colonial rule:** England

**Famous landmarks:** Mount Wilhelm, PNG's highest mountain at 4509 metres (14 794 feet), Kokoda Trail, Sepik River

**Famous people:** Sir Michael Somare (political leader)

**Traditions:** Bird of Paradise headdress, wooden masks

**Traditional food:** sweet potato, yams, sago and taro

PNG is a rugged mountainous country. Vehicles cannot reach many of the mountains and valleys. Tribes that live in these valleys do not have much contact with the outside world. These people survive by hunting and growing small patches of crops in rainforest clearings. PNG is closer to the **equator** than Australia and has a tropical climate with more rain spread over the year.

This Papua New Guinean man is wearing a traditional headdress.

# Solomon Islands in focus

**Official name:** Solomon Islands

**Area:** 28 450 square kilometres (10 985 square miles)

**Population:** 500 000

**Capital:** Honiara

**Major cities:** Gizo, Yandina, Aola

**Colonial rule:** England

**Famous landmarks:** Kolombangara Volcano, Malaita fishing village

**Famous people:** Sir Allan Kemakeza (political leader)

**Traditions:** playing music with bamboo pipes

**Traditional food:** yams and fish

The Solomon Islands are made up of two chains of islands to the east of PNG. The biggest island is Guadalcanal. People live mainly off fishing and some farming. Some people on smaller islands in the group still follow traditional lifestyles, such as worshipping sharks as Gods and using shells as money. Some of the Solomon Islands are low-lying and can get flooded by cyclones (hurricanes).

These villagers are from Guadalcanal in the Solomon Islands.

# Australia's future

Life in Australia is comfortable for many people with a high standard of living. Most people live near the coast and enjoy an outdoors lifestyle.

## Challenges

Most Australians are healthy and well educated. Some Aboriginal people suffer more serious health problems and do not have access to a good education. More Aboriginal people are becoming teachers and health workers, and then return to their communities to share their skills. It is hoped that this will help improve the lives of the people in Aboriginal communities.

Australia has some environmental problems. Many years ago, trees were chopped down to make room for farming. Clearing land in some places makes salty underground water come to the surface. This is called salinity. Where there is salt on the surface, crops cannot grow. Australia's biggest river system, the Murray–Darling, is in danger of drying up because too much water is being taken out for irrigation on farms. Scientists are looking at ways of saving Australia's rivers.

 The Swan River in Perth sometimes gets **algae** blooms that kill fish.

# Goals

Australia is rich in wildlife and beautiful scenery. One of Australia's goals is to develop industries and farming that bring in money and also look after the natural environment. Australia has formed national parks and marine parks to protect the plants and animals in some regions. In these parks people are not allowed to clear the land of trees or hunt animals. The numbat, a small Australian marsupial, is protected in national parks.

Kangaroos are protected in this national park in central Australia.

## Living together

Australia is populated by people from many different countries. Australian people that come from Asia, Europe, Africa and other countries make Australia a multicultural society. The goal is to allow people of all backgrounds to live in peace and harmony.

People from different countries live together in Australia.

# Australia in review

Australia is the smallest continent.

**Area:** 7 686 850 square kilometres (3 million square miles)

**Population:** 20 million

**First humans in Australia:** 40 000 years ago

**First civilisations:** Aboriginal and Torres Strait Islander people

**Countries:** one

**States:** six

**Territories:** two

**Highest point:** Mount Kosciuszko at 2229 metres (7313 feet)

**Longest river:** Murray–Darling River at 3750 kilometres (2330 miles)

**Climate zones:** arid, Mediterranean, tropical, temperate, alpine

**Official language:** English

**Other languages:** Italian, Greek, Aboriginal languages

## Websites

For more information on Australia go to:
http://www.worldatlas.com/webimage/countrys/au.htm

# Glossary

**algae**  a type of plant-like organism that grows in water

**alpine**  a cold, snowy climate in high mountainous regions

**ancestors**  relatives from the past

**arid**  a dry, desert-like climate

**Buddhism**  a religion where people follow the teachings of Buddha

**bush tucker**  food found in the bush and eaten by Australian Aboriginal people

**coral atolls**  small islands formed on coral reefs

**Dreamtime**  a period during which Australian Aboriginals believe that ancestral beings created the land and law

**equator**  an imaginary line around the middle of the Earth's surface

**extinct**  when no more of a particular species of plant or animal are left on the Earth

**Hinduism**  an Indian religion that worships one God through many statues called deities

**hydropower**  power made by fast-flowing water

**Judaism**  a religion followed by Jewish people

**independent**  a country that governs itself

**Islam**  a religion that worships one God called Allah and the messages God told to Muhammed

**mammals**  animals with fur that raise their young with milk

**mangroves**  trees that partly grow in salty water

**marsupials**  mammals that rear their young in a pouch

**Mediterranean**  a climate of hot dry summers and mild wet winters

**migrants**  people who move to another country to live

**outback**  land in Australia a long way from big cities

**resources**  what a country has that is valuable

**Southern Hemisphere**  the bottom half of the world below the equator

**tectonic plates**  large pieces of the Earth's crust that move slowly, causing earthquakes

**temperate**  a mild climate with wet weather and cool temperatures

**Torres Strait Islanders**  Indigenous Australians from the Torres Strait Islands area, between northern Queensland and New Guinea

**tropical**  a hot, humid and wet climate found near the equator

**wombat**  a chunky marsupial that looks like a small bear

# Index

**A**

Aboriginal people  7, 9, 16, 17, 19, 28, 30

animals  6, 14–15, 29

  budgerigar  14

  cockatoo  14

  diprotodon  6

  echidna  14

  kangaroo  6, 15, 29

  koala  14

  numbat  29

  platypus  14

  possum  6, 14

  thylacine  6

  wombat  6

**B**

borders  4

**C**

Christianity  17

climate  12–13

colonies  18, 21, 23, 25, 27

Cook, Captain James  18

coral reefs  11, 21

**D**

deserts  9, 10, 12, 15, 18

Dreamtime  17

**E**

ethnic groups  16

**F**

Fiji  20, 24, 25

**G**

Gondwana  5

**L**

lakes  7, 9, 11, 23

land ownership  19

languages  7, 9, 17, 22, 24, 26

Laurasia  5

**M**

mangroves  9

marine parks  29

migrants  9, 16, 17

mountains  4, 9, 10, 20, 22, 23, 25, 27, 30

**N**

national parks  29

New Zealand  16, 19, 20, 22–3

**O**

oceans  4, 8, 20

**P**

Pacific Region  4, 20, 22, 24, 26

Pangaea  5, 6

Papua New Guinea  19, 20, 26, 27

plants  14–15

  everlastings  15

  karri  14

**R**

religion  9, 17, 21, 22, 24, 26

rivers  9, 11, 16, 20, 27, 28, 30

**S**

salinity  28

Solomon Islands  20, 26, 27

**T**

Torres Strait Islander people  16, 17, 30

tropical rainforest  15, 27

**V**

Vanuatu  20, 24, 25

**W**

World War II  19